THIS CANDLEWICK BOOK BELONGS TO:

_____

_____

_____

For Dad and Patti, in honor of their five- 🐗 anniversary.
A. P. S. & J. S.

The dogs are for Mom; the rest of the book is for Roy.
R. C.

Text copyright © 2003 by April Pulley Sayre and Jeff Sayre
Illustrations copyright © 2003 by Randy Cecil

First paperback edition 2006

The Library of Congress has cataloged the hardcover edition as follows:

Sayre, April Pulley.
One is a snail, ten is a crab : a counting by feet book / April Pulley Sayre
and Jeff Sayre ; illustrated by Randy Cecil. —1st ed.
p.   cm.
ISBN 978-0-7636-1406-5 (hardcover)
1. Counting—Juvenile literature. 2. Foot—Juvenile literature.
I. Title: One is a snail, ten is a crab. II. Sayre, Jeff, date. III. Cecil, Randy. IV. Title.
QA113.S367 2003   2001052494

ISBN 978-0-7636-2631-0 (paperback)

18 19 20 21 22 CCP 20 19 18 17 16

Printed in Shenzhen, Guangdong, China

This book was typeset in Maiandra.
The illustrations were done in oil on paper.

Candlewick Press
99 Dover Street
Somerville, Massachusetts 02144

visit us at www.candlewick.com

One Is a Snail
Ten Is a Crab

A Counting by Feet Book

April Pulley Sayre and Jeff Sayre

illustrated by Randy Cecil

CANDLEWICK PRESS

1 is a snail.

(This is a snail's foot.)

2 is a person.

3 is a person
and a snail.

5 is a dog and a snail.

6 is an insect.

7 is an insect and a snail.

8
is a spider.

9 is a spider and a snail.

20 is two crabs.

30 is three crabs...

Or ten people and a crab.

or ten dogs.

50 is five crabs...

Or ten dogs and a crab.

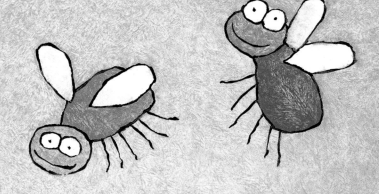

Or ten insects.

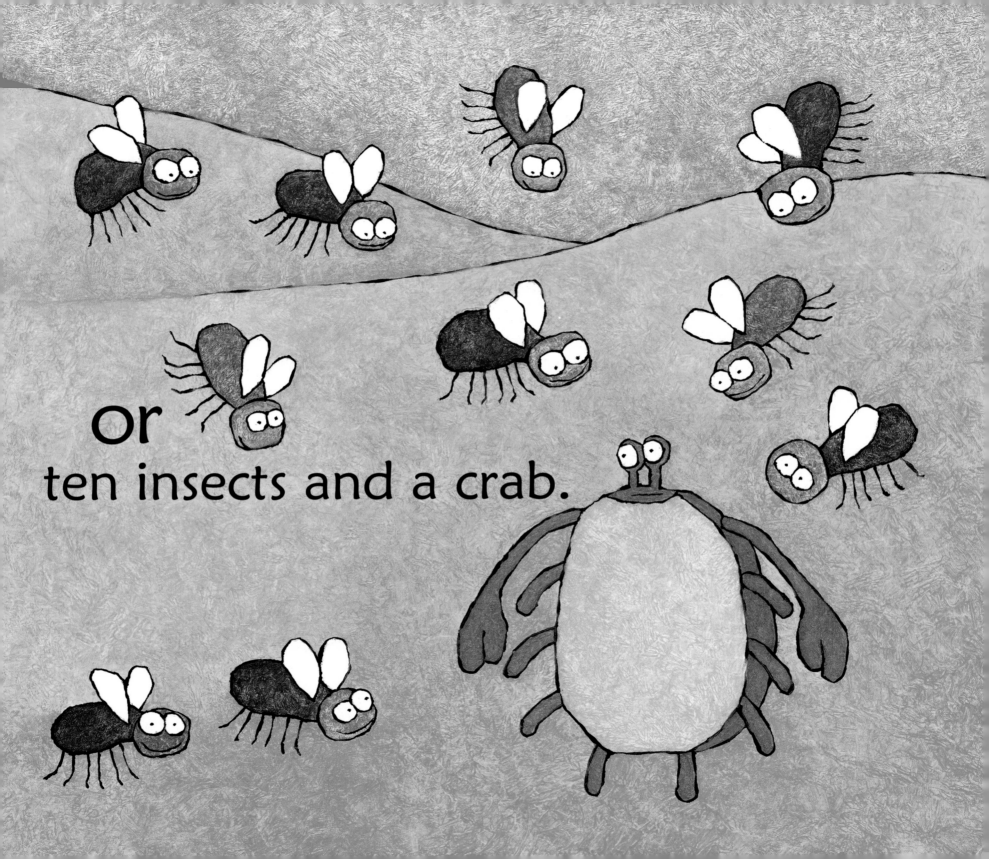

or ten insects and a crab.

80 is eight crabs...

or ten spiders.

90 is nine crabs...

or
ten spiders and a crab.

So,
100
is ten crabs...

Or, if you're really counting slowly...

one hundred snails!

April Pulley Sayre and **Jeff Sayre** are a husband-and-wife team who lead ecotours and who travel extensively to study, photograph, and film animals. They also speak at schools, botanical gardens, zoos, and nature festivals. Together they wrote *Hummingbirds: The Sun Catchers,* an adult natural history book. Jeff Sayre is an ecologist specializing in native plants and birds. April Pulley Sayre is an award-winning author of more than forty books for children, including *If You Should Hear a Honey Guide* and *Dig, Wait, Listen: A Desert Toad's Tale.* The Sayres love to brainstorm together — which is how the idea for this book came about.

Randy Cecil was born in Houston, Texas, and lives there today. He graduated from the Rhode Island School of Design and is the illustrator of numerous books for children, including *We've All Got Bellybuttons!* by David Martin and *And Here's to You!* by David Elliott. He says of *One Is a Snail,* "It was great fun to figure out how these strange creatures would react in all these different combinations. Crabs seem to have the best time together."